PARACORD
CRITTERS

Animal Shaped
Knots & Ties

Other Knot Books
By JD of *Tying It All Together*

Decorative Fusion Knots

Paracord Fusion Ties - Volume 1

Paracord Fusion Ties - Volume 2

Paracord Project Inspirations

PARACORD CRITTERS

Animal Shaped Knots & Ties

By JD of *Tying It All Together*

4th Level Indie

Paracord Critters
by J.D. Lenzen
ISBN: 978-0-9855578-9-8

Published by 4th Level Indie
Author's Site: fusionknots.com

Printed in the United States by BPR Book Group.

Distributed by Itasca Books Distribution.

Contents

Getting Started

Acknowledgments..............vii

Introduction ix

About Paracord xi

About This Book..................xiii

Twists & Terms....................xvii

Instructions

Trilobite 1

Millipede 5

Barnacle....................................9

Butterfly 15

Dragonfly 21

Rock Crab 27

Lobster Tail 35

Tree Snake 41

Bumblebee 47

Jellyfish....................................55

Octopus 63

Sea Turtle................................69

Author Info

About the Author................79

Acknowledgments

For their support and/or inspiration in the production of this book, I would like to thank Clifford W. Ashley, my parents (Jim and Barbara), Ash Gerry, Mike Stern, Steve Davis, Dale Gillespie, Ashley Somers, the subscribers to my *Tying It All Together* YouTube channel, and the members of the fusion knotting community as a whole. Without you, especially those who continue to support my online videos, this book would not have come to be.

And…

A very special thanks to my wife and muse, Kristen Kakos. Your presence in my life brings me joy, comfort, and the freedom to create. For these gifts I am forever grateful.

Introduction

Between the fall of 1994 and the spring of 1996, I was living a very different life than the one I am today. I was in my early twenties, fresh out of college, and working as a naturalist at Exploring New Horizons (ENH), an outdoor education school in Loma Mar, California. Nestled between the coastal town of Pescadero and the mountain top town of La Honda, Loma Mar was my home, the place that I lived and worked, and a place that I loved.

Loma Mar's towering redwoods, multitude of plants, diversity of animals (including insects), and the winding Pescadero Creek that flows through it, all felt like friends to me. Friends that I visited, studied, and introduced to rotating groups of students, week after week.

Nearly twenty years later, I'm still working as an educator. Only now, I teach others how to make classic and original knots and ties with paracord. The knots and ties that I teach, through my hundreds of YouTube videos (youtube.com/TyingItAllTogether) and multiple instruction books, are often inspired by significant life experiences. So it is, *Paracord Critters* (PC) was inspired by my days living and working as a naturalist.

Combining my knowledge and appreciation of animals with my knowledge and appreciation of knots and ties, PC features twelve step-by-step instructions for critters that live underwater, on land, and in the sky—with each creation represented as a useful item (pin, key fob, necklace) or figurine.

So grab a couple of lengths of paracord, find a comfortable place to sit, and work your way through the diversity of knots and ties presented in this book. Or better yet, make these knots and ties outdoors. Who knows? The experience might inspire you to design a few new paracord critters on your own!

JD of *Tying It All Together*

About Paracord

Background

Paracord is a lightweight nylon rope constructed with a core of yarns wrapped in a woven exterior sheath. The word *paracord* derives from its original use as suspension lines for U.S. parachutes during World War II. This said, on account of paracord's utility, paratroopers used it for a variety of other tasks once on the ground.

As with other materials and technologies originally slated for military use, paracord has since become widely valued in civilian circles. Its commercial availability (not surprisingly) was initially pressed forward by military veterans who'd grown accustomed to its use during service. Over the years, support for its availability has been equally heralded by gun and knife collectors, hunters, survivalists, do-it-yourself (DIY) makers, as well as an ever-growing community of paracord crafters.

Types

The U.S. military describes six types of paracord (Type I, IA, II, IIA, III and IV). However, for the purposes of the information provided in this book and the fundamental "need to know" knowledge of the readers, paracord is generally available in two forms, Type II and III. Type II paracord is conventionally called 450 paracord (minimum strength 450 pounds) and usually has a core consisting of 4 two-ply yarns. Type III paracord is referred to as 550 paracord (minimum strength 550 pounds) and typically has a core consisting of 7 two-ply yarns.

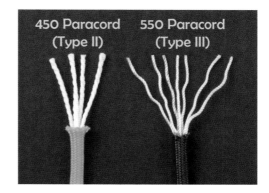

The ties presented in this book were created with 450 paracord. I used 450 paracord because I enjoy its pliability (it's very amenable to fusion knotting techniques) and the variety of colors it comes in. However, 550 paracord and a wide variety of other cord types could be used to create all the designs shown in this book. In short, when in doubt, give it a tie!

About This Book

Instruction Format

The intent of this book is to provide all the information necessary to successfully complete each knot or tie presented while minimizing the description of repetitive procedures. For example, procedures performed on every knot or tie, such as snipping and singeing, are shown only once (see Page xiv) and then simply referenced as a procedure to be performed in the instruction text (i.e., "Carefully snip and singe the cord ends.").

In cases where a knot is repeatedly used, such as the 2-Strand Diamond Knot and the 8-Strand Diamond Knot, the instruction text calls out the knot to be tied accompanied by the page number where that knot was first shown.

When the instruction text contains left and right cords that perform all required actions and remain outside the placement of the middle cords, the terms "left running end" and "right running end" are used. If, on the other hand, the left and right cords swap position with the middle cords, the terms "leftmost cord" and "rightmost cord" are used.

Snipping, Singeing, & Shaping

Paracord is made of nylon, and nylon is a thermoplastic (also known as a thermosoftening plastic). Put another way, nylon is a polymer that turns into a liquid when heated. During this heated state it can be molded.

When it comes to snipping and singeing the ends of paracord, this molding "glasses" the ends of the cord. This change in physical state seals paracord ends until a greater (human sourced) force is applied (i.e., the flared ends are pulled through the cinched loop and/or the glassed ends are broken).

When shaping paracord, heat helps fix a cord form in place (e.g., helps hold the look of curved or curled jellyfish tentacles).

> **WARNING:** Children should not use shears (i.e., scissors) or lighters without adult supervision. If you're reading this, and you're not sure if this warning applies to you…it probably does. Stop, show the following instructions to a competent parent or guardian, and ask for their assistance.

About This Book

How to Snip & Singe Cord Ends

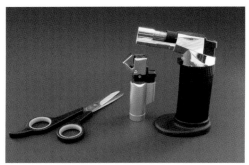

1. Begin with the possession of the following items: **Barber Shears** and a **Butane Torch Lighter**

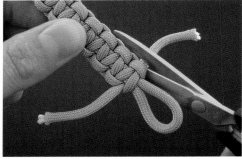

2. Once the desired tie length is achieved, carefully snip the undesired cord ends off with your shears.

3. Once the undesired cord ends are removed…

4. …ready your lighter. Make sure to keep hands away from the lighter tip.

About This Book

How to Snip & Singe Cord Ends (continued)

5. Quickly (no more than 1 to 2 seconds) singe the first snipped end of your cord…

6. …and then the second. While the "glassed" ends of your snipped paracord are still soft…

7. …but no longer hot to the touch, mold them with your thumb.

8. Congratulations, you've successfully sealed the ends of your paracord tie in place!

About This Book

How to (Help) Fix a Cord Form

1. Some book critters have paracord "tentacles" (like the jellyfish) or "arms" and "tentacles" (like the octopus).

2. To help fix a dynamic curve or curl in these critter body parts, twist or coil the paracord (twisting shown).

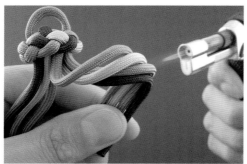

3. Then quickly (no more than 1 to 2 seconds) singe the arches of the twisted or coiled cords.

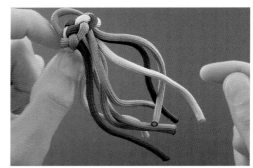

4. This will (help) fix the cord forms in place (in this case jellyfish tentacles) by "glassing" the bent paracord.

Twists & Terms

The following visual clarifications and definitions are meant to provide an understanding of the knotting procedures and terms associated with this book.

Visual Clarifications

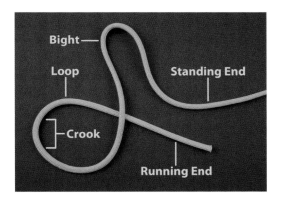

Cord Parts

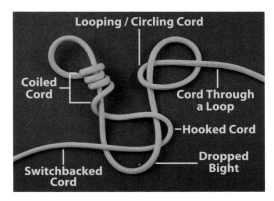

Cord Loops

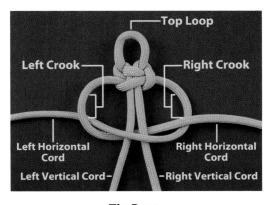

Tie Parts

Tie Movements

Twists & Terms

Definitions

ABOK: Acronym for *The Ashley Book of Knots*.

Apex: The top or highest part of an object.

Bight: A line doubled over into a U-shape.

Carapace: A hard shell on the back of some animals (e.g., rock crab and turtle).

Circle: A line making one complete revolution around another line or body part (e.g., finger).

Clockwise Loop: A loop that has a running end (or line on top) that rotates clockwise.

Cord: A slender length of flexible material used to make a knot or tie.

Counterclockwise Loop: A loop that has a running end (or line on top) that rotates counterclockwise.

Crook: The curved inside part of a bight, circle, loop, or hooked line.

DFK: Acronym for the book *Decorative Fusion Knots*.

Figurine: A small representation of a human, deity, or animal.

Firm: The point at which the adjusting of a knot results in a satisfactory appearance.

Flip: Turning a knot, tie, or semi-completed knot or tie over, upside down, vertically, or horizontally.

Fusion Tie: An innovative tie created through the merging of different knot elements or knotting techniques.

Historical Tie: A tie that was discovered or created before 1979 (the year the IGKT updated ABOK).

Hook: A line that makes a sharp curve or a shape resembling a hook, typically around a line.

Horizontal: Referring to a flat or level position.

IGKT: Acronym for the International Guild of Knot Tyers.

Invertebrate: An animal lacking a backbone.

Key Fob: A generally decorative, at times

Twists & Terms

useful, item or tie that connects to a key ring or key.

Legs: Dangling or vertical parallel cords.

Line: The material used to tie a knot or tie (e.g., paracord, rope, wire, etc.).

Loop: A circle of line that crosses itself, or a bight cinched at its base.

Nub: A small lump or protuberance.

P: A line that is looped to look like the letter P or the mirror image of the letter P.

Paracord: A lightweight nylon rope constructed with a core of yarns wrapped in a woven exterior sheath.

PC: Acronym for the book *Paracord Critters*.

Pendant: A piece of jewelry, knot, or tie that hangs from a line worn around the neck.

PFT-V1: Acronym for the book *Paracord Fusion Ties - Volume 1*.

PFT-V2: Acronym for the book *Paracord Fusion Ties - Volume 2*.

Piece: The partially completed or final version of an entire knot or tie.

PPI: Acronym for the book *Paracord Project Inspirations*.

Running End: The end of a line that is being used to make the knot or tie.

Singe: Scorching the end of a cut line to hold it in place or keep it from fraying.

Standing End: The end of a line that is not involved in making the knot or tie.

TIAT: Acronym for the YouTube video channel *Tying It All Together*.

Tuck: Inserting a line or bight through a loop or under another line.

U: A line that is shaped to look like the letter U.

Vertical: Referring to an upright position, at a right angle to the horizon.

X: Two lines or sets of lines that cross over one another in the configuration of the letter X.

TRILOBITE

Trilobites are extinct marine invertebrates that once lived in every ocean of the ancient world. Represented in knotted form by their multiple articulated body segments, similar imprints can be seen in their fossilized remains.

Cord Used: One 4 ft. (1.2 m) Cord = 1.5 in. (3.8 cm) Long, Key Fob
Challenge Level: Beginner
Origin: Historical Tie

1. Bight the middle of the cord down 4.5 in. (11.3 cm).

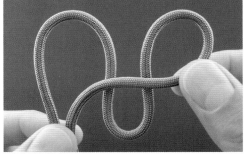

2. Hook the right running end left, over the middlemost vertical cords.

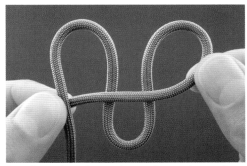

3. Drop the left running end over the cord beneath it.

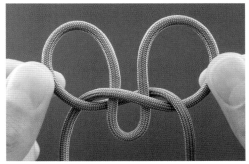

4. Then hook it right, under the vertical cords, and through the back of the right loop.

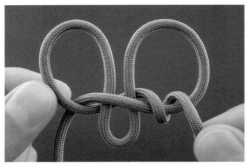

5. Circle the right running end around the right side of the loop above it.

6. Circle the left running end around the left side of the loop above it.

7. Extend the left running end right, under the vertical cords, and through the back of the right loop.

8. Extend the right running end left, over the vertical cords, and through the front of the left loop.

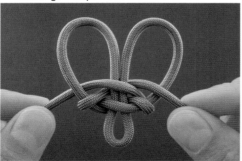

9. Adjust the piece until its width is approximately 1.5 in. (3.8 cm).

10. Repeat Steps 5 through 9 six more times.

11. Tighten up the piece by pulling the running ends and the standing (loop) end apart, firmly.

12. Carefully snip and singe the running ends, 0.5 in. (1.3 cm) from their base, to complete the Trilobite Key Fob.

Millipede

Millipedes are land-based invertebrates with two pairs of legs on (most of) their body segments. The Latin roots of the word *millipede* are "thousand" and "foot." Still, no millipede actually has 1,000 legs and the tie below limits its leg count to 25.

Cord Used: *One 10 ft. (3 m) Cord = 7 in. (17.8 cm) Long, Figurine*
Challenge Level: *Beginner*
Origin: *Historical Tie*

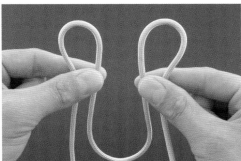

1. Bight the middle of the cord down 8.5 in. (21.6 cm).

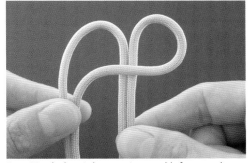

2. Hook the right running end left, over the middlemost vertical cords.

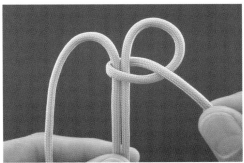

3. Then hook it right, under the vertical cords, and through the back of the right crook.

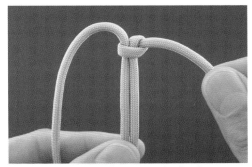

4. Tighten the Half Hitch made, firmly.

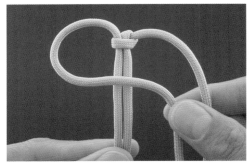

5. Hook the left running end right, over the middlemost vertical cords.

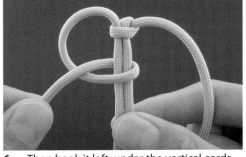

6. Then hook it left, under the vertical cords, and through the back of the left crook.

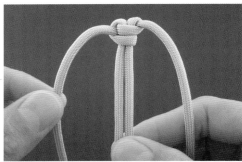

7. Tighten the Half Hitch made, firmly.

8. Repeat Steps 2 through 7 until 1.5 in. (3.8 cm) of loop length remains.

9. Carefully snip and singe the horizontal cord ends, at their base.

10. Shape the piece, arching the Half Hitches toward the snipped and singed cord ends.

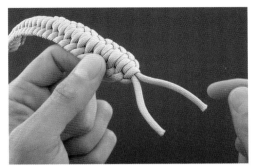

11. Carefully snip the loop end in half.

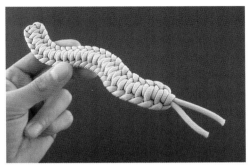

12. Then carefully singe the exposed cord ends to complete the Millipede Figurine.

BARNACLE

Barnacles start their lives swimming in water before gluing their heads to a surface, secreting calcium-hard plates, and using their feet to feed. This life cycle makes them, and their knotted representation, one of my favorite critters in this book.

Cord Used: *One 6 ft. (1.8 m) Cord = 1 in. (2.5 cm) Dia., Pendant*
Challenge Level: *Novice*
Origin: *Fusion Tie*

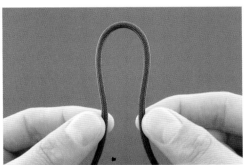

1. Approximately 10 in. (25.4 cm) right of the middle of the cord, make a bight.

2. Rotate the bight into a clockwise loop.

3. Bight the right running end through the loop…

4. …and tighten, leaving a 0.5 in. (1.3 cm) loop in the Slip Knot made.

5. Pull the loop of the Slip Knot out 4 in. (10.2 cm).

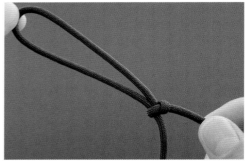

6. Flip the piece over, horizontally.

7. Tilt the loop right until it's horizontal. The long cord end should remain below.

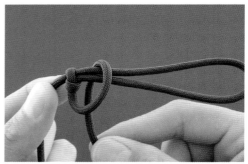

8. Hook the long cord/running end up, over the horizontal cords.

9. Then hook it down, under the horizontal cords, and through the back of the crook below.

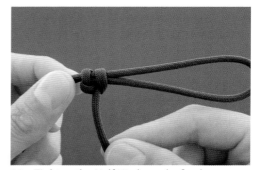

10. Tighten the Half Hitch made, firmly.

11. Hook the running end up, under the horizontal cords.

12. Then hook it down, over the horizontal cords, and through the front of the crook below.

13. Tighten the Half Hitch made, firmly.

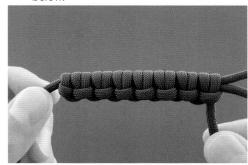

14. Repeat Steps 8 through 13 six more times.

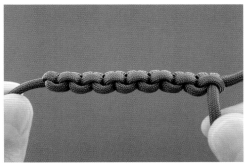

15. Rotate the piece vertically until the (right) running end is facing you.

16. Arch the right and left side of the piece up until a **U** forms.

17. Then insert the left running end through the loop.

18. Insert the right running end through the loop, exiting over the left running end.

19. Pull on the left running end (now on the right side of the piece)…

20. …until the Barnacle Pendant circles closed firmly. Leave the cords long for a necklace.

BUTTERFLY

Butterflies can breathe through their abdomen, fly up to 12 miles per hour, and taste with their feet, all while looking astonishingly beautiful. The butterfly tie symbolizes this wondrous insect by emulating its delicate silhouette.

Cord Used: *One 4 ft. (1.2 m) Cord = 1.5 in. (3.8 cm) Tall, Hair Clip or Brooch*
Challenge Level: *Novice*
Origin: *Fusion Tie*

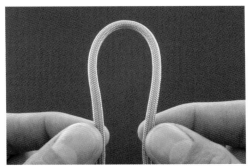

1. At the middle of the cord, make a bight.

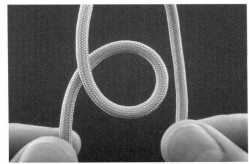

2. **2-Strand Diamond Knot:** One inch (2.5 cm) below the bight, make a clockwise **P** with the left cord.

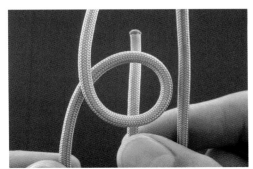

3. Lift the right running end up, behind the loop of the **P**.

4. Drop the running end down, over the cord above the **P**, and under the "leg" of the **P**.

5. Bight the running end and weave it over, under, and over the cords to the right.

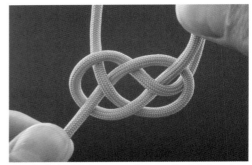

6. Pull the bight out to form a Carrick Bend.

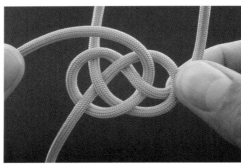

7. Now, hook the right running end left, over the (left) cord above the Carrick Bend…

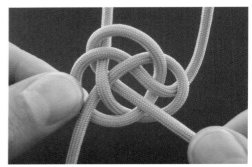

8. …and insert it through the (back) center of the Carrick Bend.

9. Then hook the left running end right, under the other running end, and over the (right) cord above the Carrick Bend…

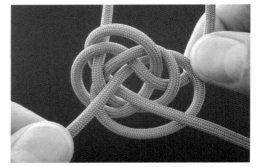

10. …and insert it through the (back) center of the Carrick Bend.

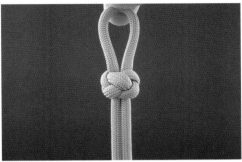

11. Adjust the cord ends until a firm and symmetrical 2-Strand Diamond Knot is formed.

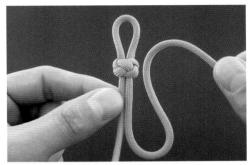

12. Bight the right vertical cord down approximately 2.5 in. (6.4 cm).

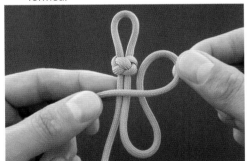

13. Then make a clockwise loop with its end, hooking it left.

14. Bight the left vertical cord down, approximately 2.5 in. (6.4 cm) under the front horizontal cord.

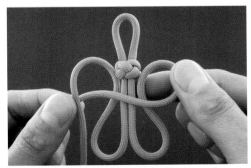

15. Then drop it over the front horizontal cord.

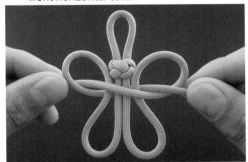

16. Now hook it right, under the vertical cords, and through the back of the right loop.

Paracord Critters

17. Hook the cord exiting the left loop right, over the vertical bights.

18. Drop the cord exiting the right loop over the cord beneath it.

19. Then hook it left, under the vertical bights, and through the back of the lower left crook.

20. Tighten the piece until firm, leaving 0.75 in. (1.9 cm) loops on top and 0.5 in. (1.3 cm) loops on bottom.

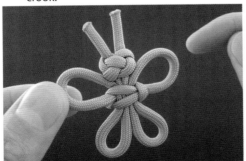

21. Carefully snip and singe the horizontal cord ends, at their base.

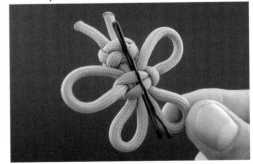

22. To fix the Butterfly to hair or attach it to an object, slide a hair pin or a safety pin under its back knot.

DRAGONFLY

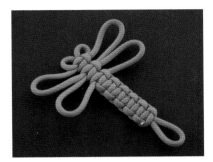

Dragonflies, like their associated tie, represent success, victory, and happiness in Japan. Characterized by large eyes, long paired wings, and elongated bodies, they can fly backwards and hover in midair for up to a minute.

Cord Used: *One 6 ft. (1.8 m) Cord = 3 in. (7.6 cm) Long, Key Fob*
Challenge Level: *Novice*
Origin: *Historical Tie*

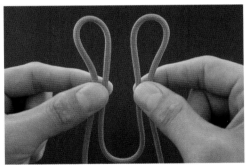

1. Bight the middle of the cord down 4 in. (10.2 cm).

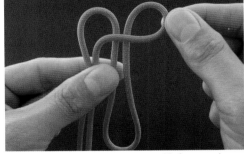

2. Hook the right running end left, over the middlemost vertical cords.

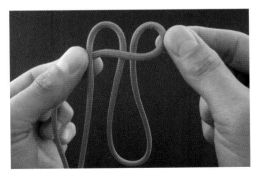

3. Drop the left running end over the cord beneath it.

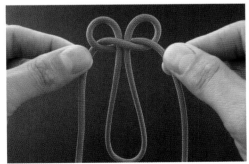

4. Then hook it right, under the vertical cords, and through the back of the right crook.

5. Hook the left running end right, over the vertical cords.

6. Drop the right running end over the cord beneath it. Then hook it left, under the vertical cords…

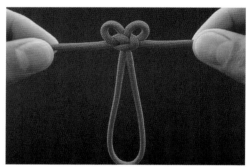

7. …and through the back of the left crook, leaving 0.25 in. (0.64 cm) loops above. Tighten firmly.

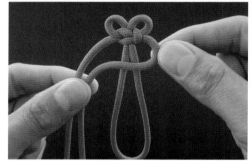

8. Hook the right running end left, over the vertical cords.

9. Drop the left running end over the cord beneath it.

10. Then hook it right, under the vertical cords, and through the back of the right crook.

11. Hook the left running end right, over the vertical cords.

12. Drop the right running end over the cord beneath it.

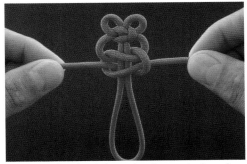

13. Then hook it left, under the vertical cords, and through the back of the left crook.

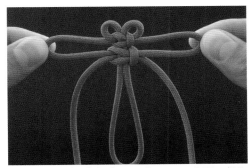

14. Pull each of the loops above out 1.5 in. (3.8 cm), horizontally.

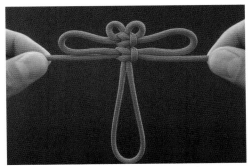

15. Then tighten the knot below firmly.

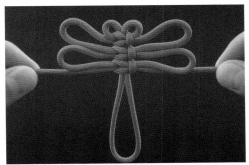

16. Repeat Steps 8 through 15 one more time.

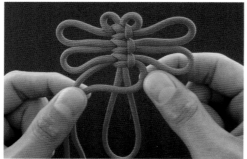

17. Hook the right running end left, over the vertical cords.

18. Drop the left running end over the cord beneath it.

19. Then hook it right, under the vertical cords, and through the back of the right crook.

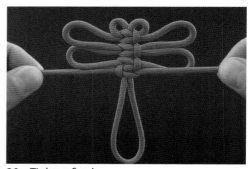

20. Tighten firmly.

21. Hook the left running end right, over the vertical cords.

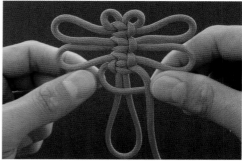

22. Drop the right running end over the cord beneath it.

23. Then hook it left, under the vertical cords, and through the back of the left crook.

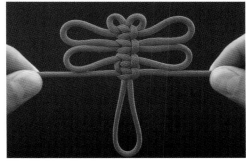

24. Tighten firmly.

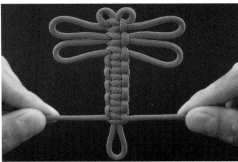

25 Repeat Steps 17 through 24 until 1 in. (2.5 cm) of loop length remains.

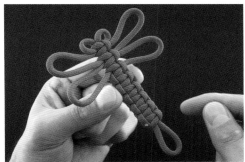

26. Carefully snip and singe the horizontal cord ends, at their base, to complete the Dragonfly Fob.

ROCK CRAB

Rock crabs are common intertidal critters I routinely saw scurrying about rocky Pacific shorelines, back when I worked as a naturalist. Their tie represents the animal's most notable features, the carapace and claws.

Cord Used: Three 3 ft. (0.9 m) Cords = 1.5 in. (3.8 cm) Tall, Key Fob
Challenge Level: Intermediate
Origin: Fusion Tie

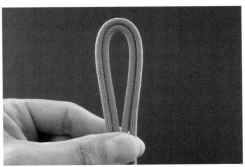

1. Start with bights created at the middle of two cords.

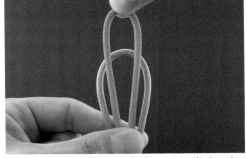

2. Drop one of the cords down 1 in. (2.5 cm) behind the bight of the other.

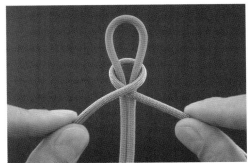

3. Cross the back cords over the front (vertical) cords, right over left.

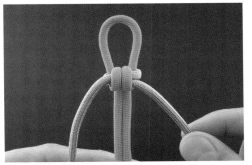

4. Circle the vertical cords around the crossed cords, between the legs above.

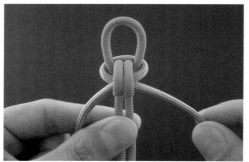

5. Leaving a 1 in. (2.5 cm) bight on top, pull the right and left horizontal cords out.

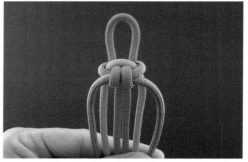

6. Lace the third cord over the vertical cords and through the loop of the horizontal cords. Stop at its middle.

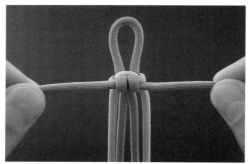

7. Tighten the right and left horizontal cords over the third cord.

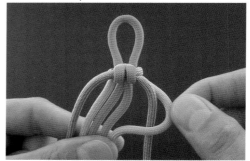

8. Hook the rightmost vertical cord left, over the right horizontal cord.

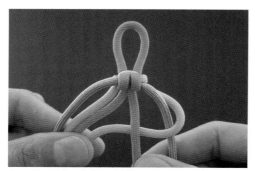

9. Drop the right middlemost vertical cord over the cord beneath it.

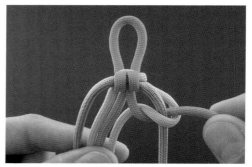

10. Then hook it right, under the (now) rightmost vertical cord, and through the back of the right crook.

Rock Crab

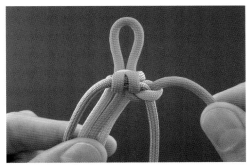

11. Tighten firmly.

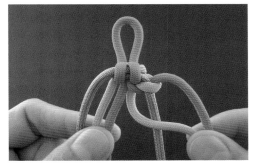

12. Hook the (now) horizontal cord, left of the rightmost vertical cord, right, over the vertical cord.

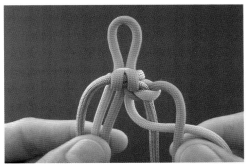

13. Drop the (now) horizontal cord, right of the rightmost vertical cord, over the cord beneath it.

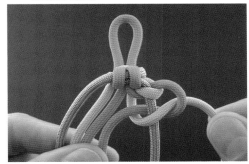

14. Then hook it left, under the vertical cord, and through the back of the left crook.

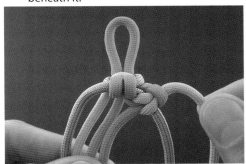

15. Tighten firmly.

16. Repeat Steps 8 through 15 two more times.

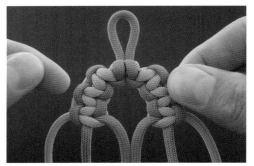

17. Repeat Steps 8 through 15 around the leftmost horizontal cord, in reflection of the right side of the piece.

18. Flip the piece over, horizontally. Then hook the middlemost horizontal cords right and left, over the vertical cords.

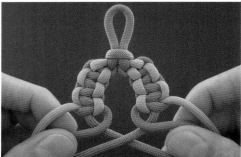

19. Cross the vertical cords, right over left.

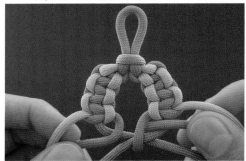

20. Circle the right middlemost horizontal cord around the crossed cords, outside the leg above.

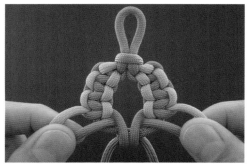

21. Circle the left middlemost horizontal cord around the crossed cords, outside the leg above.

22. Tighten the piece until firm.

23. Hook the rightmost horizontal cord left, over the right vertical cord.

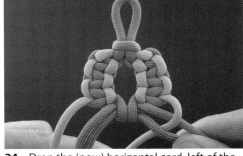

24. Drop the (now) horizontal cord, left of the right vertical cord, over the cord beneath it.

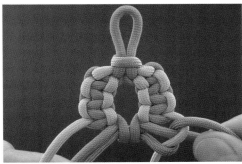

25. Then hook it right, under the vertical cord, and through the back of the right crook.

26. Tighten firmly.

27. Hook the horizontal cord, left of the right vertical cord, over the vertical cord.

28. Drop the rightmost horizontal cord over the cord beneath it.

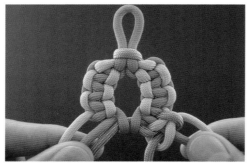

29. Then hook it left, under the vertical cord, and through the back of the left crook.

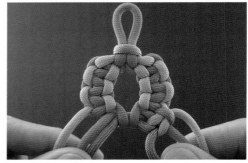

30. Tighten firmly.

31. Repeat Steps 23 through 30 around the left vertical cord, in reflection of the right side of the piece.

32. Carefully snip and singe the cord ends, at their base, to complete the Rock Crab Fob.

LOBSTER TAIL

The lobster tail tie mimics the look of a lobster's abdomen, complete with articulating segments and swimmerets. Among other things, swimmerets help lobsters move, circulate water, and help female lobsters carry and ventilate eggs.

Cord Used: One 8 ft. (2.4 m) Cord = 3.5 in. (8.9 cm) Long, Key Fob
Challenge Level: Intermediate
Origin: Fusion Tie

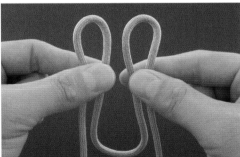

1. Bight the middle of the cord down 5 in. (12.7 cm).

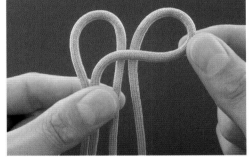

2. Hook the right running end left, over the middlemost vertical cords.

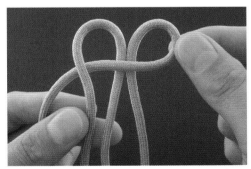

3. Drop the left running end over the cord beneath it.

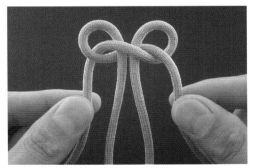

4. Then hook it right, under the vertical cords, and through the back of the right crook.

5. Tighten firmly.

6. Hook the left running end right, over and under the vertical cords.

7. Hook the right running end left, over and under the vertical cords…

8. …under the horizontal cord above it, and through the back of its crook.

9. Then circle the running end around the crook beneath it.

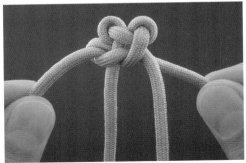

10. Adjust the cords until the knot is firm.

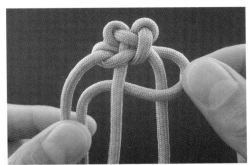

11. Hook the right running end left, over and under the vertical cords.

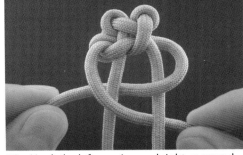

12. Hook the left running end right, over and under the vertical cords…

13. …under the horizontal cord above it, and through the back of its crook.

14. Then circle the running end around the crook beneath it.

15. Adjust the cords until the knot is firm.

16. Repeat Steps 6 through 15 until 1.5 in. (3.8 cm) of loop length remains.

17. Hook the left running end right, over and under the vertical cords.

18. Hook the right running end left, over and under the vertical cords…

19. …under the horizontal cord above it, and through the back of its crook.

20. Tighten firmly.

21. Carefully snip and singe the horizontal cord ends, at their base.

22. The completed Lobster Tail Fob.

TREE SNAKE

A tree snake's agility, coupled with its slender body and tail, make it relatively easy to recognize. Although featured in tie form as green, body colors vary from brown to green to olive-green to black, and sometimes even blue.

Cord Used: *One 8 ft. (2.4 m) Cord & One 10 in. (25.4 cm) Cord = 8 in. (20.3 cm) Long, Figurine*
Challenge Level: *Intermediate*
Origin: *Fusion Tie*

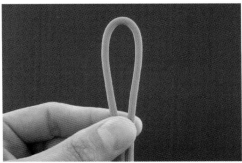

1. At the middle of the long cord, make a bight.

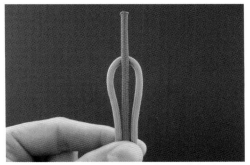

2. Line up the short cord in front of the long cord, with its end extending 1 in. (2.5 cm) above the bight.

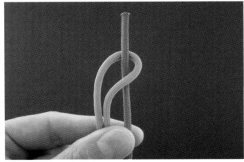

3. Hook the right running end left, over the vertical cord.

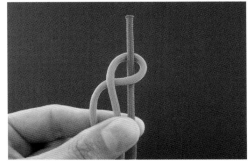

4. Drop the left running end over the cord beneath it.

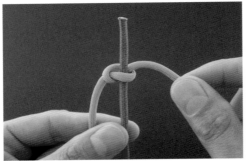

5. Then hook it right, under the vertical cord, and through the back of the right crook.

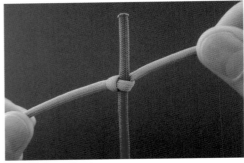

6. Tighten firmly.

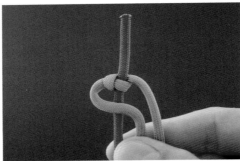

7. Hook the left running end right, over the vertical cord.

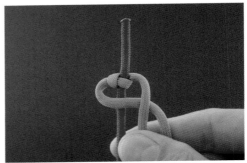

8. Drop the right running end over the cord beneath it.

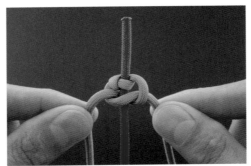

9. Then hook it left, under the vertical cord, and through the back of the left crook.

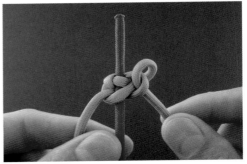

10. Circle the right running end around the crook beneath it.

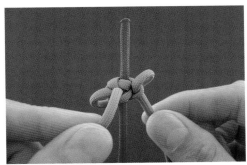

11. Circle the left running end around the crook beneath it.

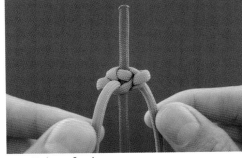

12. Tighten firmly.

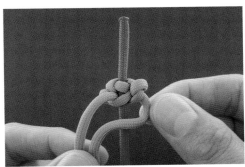

13. Hook the right running end left, over the vertical cord.

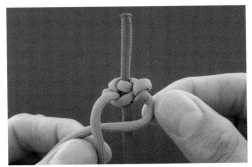

14. Drop the left running end over the cord beneath it.

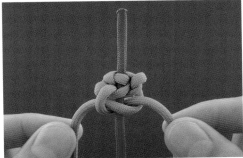

15. Then hook it right, under the vertical cord, and through the back of the right crook.

16. Tighten firmly.

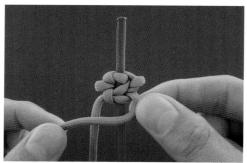

17. Hook the right running end left, over the vertical cord and the left running end.

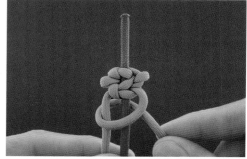

18. Then hook it right, around the back of all cords, making a counterclockwise loop.

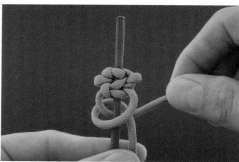

19. Hook the left running end right, under all cords, including the leg of the looped cord.

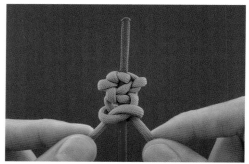

20. Then hook it left, over the front of the looped cord and through its counterclockwise loop.

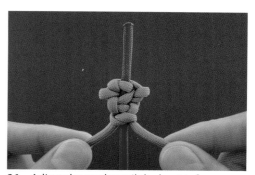

21. Adjust the cords until the knot is firm.

22. Repeat Steps 17 through 21 until 1 in. (2.5 cm) of the middlemost cord remains.

23. Carefully snip and singe the middlemost cord end, at its base, and the outer cord ends, 1 in. (2.5 cm) from their base.

24. The completed Tree Snake Figurine.

BUMBLEBEE

Bumblebees pollinate more plants, more efficiently, over more areas of the world than honeybees do. They're critical to the survival of vegetables, fruits, and certain grains, and well deserve the reproduction of their likeness in knotted form.

Cord Used: *One 5 ft. (1.5 m) Cord & One 3 ft. (0.9 m) Cord = 2 in. (5.1 cm) Long, Pendant*
Challenge Level: *Advanced*
Origin: *Fusion Tie*

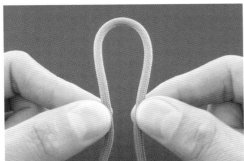

1. At the middle of the short cord, make a bight.

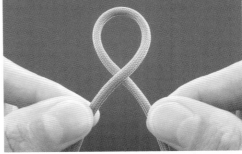

2. Rotate the bight into a clockwise loop.

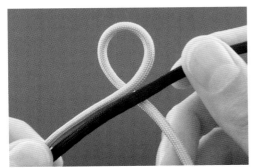

3. Then cross the middle of the long cord across the apex of the right running end.

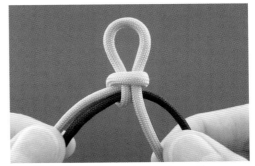

4. Bight the right running end over the second cord and through the loop.

5. Tighten the piece, leaving a 0.25 in. (0.64 cm) nub in the Slip Knot made.

6. Lift the ends of the long cord until they extend beyond the ends of the short cord.

7. Hook the right running end left, over all three vertical cords.

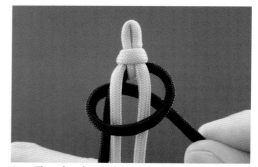

8. Then hook it right, around the back of the vertical cords, making a counterclockwise loop.

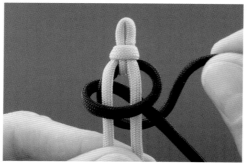

9. Hook the leftmost circled cord right, under the vertical cords and the leg of the looped cord.

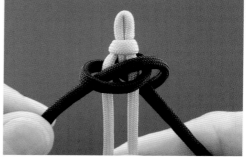

10. Then hook it left, over the front of the looped cord and through its counterclockwise loop.

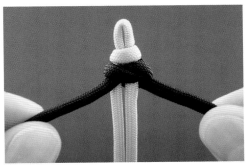

11. Adjust the cords until the knot is firm, but not too tight.

12. Lift the short cord ends until they extend beyond the long cord ends.

13. Repeat Steps 7 through 11.

14. Lift the long cord ends until they extend beyond the short cord ends.

15. Repeat Steps 7 through 11.

16. Hook the right middlemost cord left, over the left middlemost cord.

17. Then hook it right, around the back of the left middlemost cord, making a counterclockwise loop.

18. Hook the circled cord right, under the leg of the looped cord.

19. Then hook it left, over the front of the looped cord and through its counterclockwise loop.

20. Insert the right (long) cord through the right loop of the knot below.

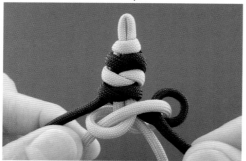

21. Then circle it around the right side of the loop, exiting over itself.

22. Insert the left (long) cord through the left loop of the knot below.

23. Then circle it around the left side of the loop, exiting over itself.

24. Adjust the short cords until the knot is firm, leaving 0.5 in. (1.3 cm) loops in the long cords.

25. Repeat Steps 7 through 11.

26. Adjust the cords until the knot is as tight as you can make it.

27. Tie a **2-Strand Diamond Knot** (see Page 15), 0.5 in. (1.3 cm) below the base of the long cords.

28. Insert the long cords through the middle of the Diamond Knot.

29. Then adjust the Diamond Knot until it presses against the base of the long cords.

30. Pull all cords firmly apart, exposing their base.

31. Carefully snip and singe the short cord ends, at their base.

32. The completed Bumblebee Necklace.

JELLYFISH

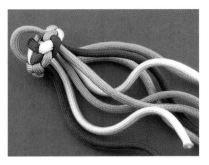

Jellyfish are relatively simple creatures. Lacking brains, blood, or even hearts, they free-swim through the ocean using their tentacles to capture and eat tiny plants and animals they can't actually see. Ironically, their namesake tie is more "advanced."

Cord Used: *Four 2 ft. (0.6 m) Cords = 4 in. (10.2 cm) Long, Key Fob*
Challenge Level: *Advanced*
Origin: *Fusion Tie*

1. Cross the first cord over the second at their middles, making an **X**.

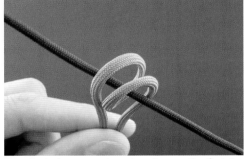

2. Arch the second cord ends over the first, in opposite directions, right cord above left.

3. Weave the lower cord end over the arch above it…

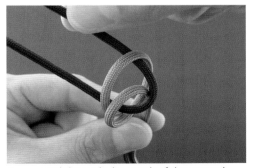

4. …and through the crook of the second arch.

5. Weave the upper cord end over the arch below it…

6. …and through the crook of the second arch, making a loosely tied Crown Knot.

7. Take the tip of the third cord in hand…

8. …and insert it through the side of the Crown Knot, stopping at the cord's middle.

9. Take the tip of the fourth cord in hand…

10. …and insert it through the side of the Crown Knot, perpendicular to the third cord, stopping at the fourth cord's middle.

11. 8-Strand Diamond Knot: Moving counter-clockwise, cross the bottom cord over the lower right cord.

12. Cross the lower right cord over the middle right cord above it.

13. Cross the middle right cord over the upper right cord above it.

14. Cross the upper right cord over the top cord.

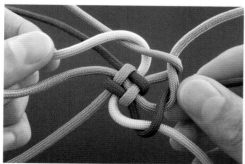

15. Cross the top cord over the upper left cord.

16. Cross the upper left cord over the middle left cord below it.

17. Cross the middle left cord over the lower left cord below it.

18. Then take the tip of the lower left cord in hand…

19. …and insert it over and through the bottom crook.

20. Adjust the cords until they fit loosely around, but do not cover, the lower Crown Knot.

21. Now, hook the bottom cord counter-clockwise, around the arched cord beside it…

22. …and insert it through the center of the upper Crown Knot.

23. Hook the next cord end (in front of the one before) counterclockwise, around the arched cord beside it…

24. …and insert it through the center of the upper Crown Knot.

25. Hook the next cord end (in front of the one before) counterclockwise, around the arched cord beside it…

26. …and insert it through the center of the upper Crown Knot.

27. Hook the next cord end (in front of the one before) counterclockwise, around the arched cord beside it…

28. …and insert it through the center of the upper Crown Knot.

Paracord Critters

29. Hook the next cord end (in front of the one before) counterclockwise, around the arched cord beside it…

30. …and insert it through the center of the upper Crown Knot.

31. Hook the next cord end (in front of the one before) counterclockwise, around the arched cord beside it…

32. …and insert it through the center of the upper Crown Knot.

33. Hook the next cord end (in front of the one before) counterclockwise, around the arched cord beside it…

34. …and insert it through the center of the upper Crown Knot.

35. Finally, hook the last cord end counter-clockwise, around the arched cord beside it…

36. …and insert it through the center of the upper Crown Knot.

37. Adjust the piece until the Diamond Knot is firm, pulling out a 0.5 in. (1.3 cm) arch in the top cord before tightening.

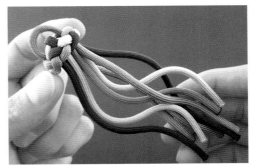

38. Carefully snip and singe the running ends, 4 in. (10.2 cm) from their base, to complete the Jellyfish Fob.

OCTOPUS

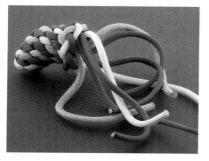

Inspiration for the mythical Kraken, and now a knotted figurine, octopuses are the brains of the underwater world. Interestingly, most of their problem solving neurons are inside their arms, allowing their arms to think independently of their heads.

Cord Used: *Four 3 ft. (0.9 m) Cords = 6 in. (15.2 cm) Long, Figurine*
Challenge Level: *Advanced*
Origin: *Fusion Tie*

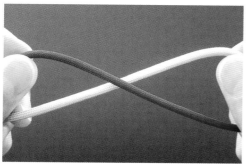

1. Cross the first cord over the second at their middles, making an **X**.

2. Arch the second cord ends over the first, in opposite directions, right cord above left.

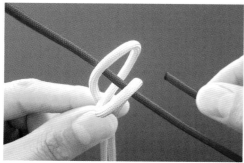

3. Weave the lower cord end over the arch above it…

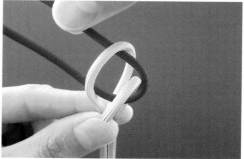

4. …and through the crook of the second arch.

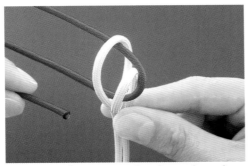

5. Weave the upper cord end over the arch below it…

6. …and through the crook of the second arch, making a loosely tied Crown Knot.

7. Take the tip of the third cord in hand…

8. …and insert it through the side of the Crown Knot, stopping at the cord's middle.

9. Take the tip of the fourth cord in hand…

10. …and insert it through the side of the Crown Knot, perpendicular to the third cord, stopping at the fourth cord's middle.

11. Moving counterclockwise, cross the bottom cord over the lower right cord.

12. Cross the lower right cord over the middle right cord above it.

13. Cross the middle right cord over the upper right cord above it.

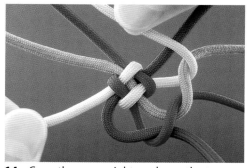

14. Cross the upper right cord over the top cord.

15. Cross the top cord over the upper left cord.

16. Cross the upper left cord over the middle left cord below it.

17. Cross the middle left cord over the lower left cord below it.

18. Then take the tip of the lower left cord in hand…

19. …and insert it over and through the bottom crook.

20. Adjust the cords until they fit snugly around, but do not cover, the lower Crown Knot.

21. Repeat Steps 11 through 20 seven more times.

22. **Note:** The center of the Octopus should be open and hollow.

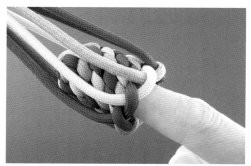

23. If it is not, use a finger to widen the center, bottom to top.

24. Tie an **8-Strand Diamond Knot** (see Page 57) with the remaining cords.

25. Use a finger to support the Octopus's center as you shape its body.

26. Carefully snip and singe the running ends, 5 in. (12.7cm) from their base, to complete the Octopus Figurine.

SEA TURTLE

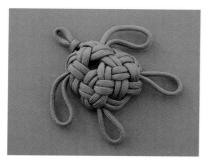

If you see a real or knotted sea turtle on a beach, odds are it's a female. Male sea turtles live their entire lives at sea, while females occasionally come ashore to lay eggs. Baby sea turtles emerge from the laid eggs about sixty days later.

Cord Used: *One 10 ft. (3 m) Cord = 3.5 in. (8.9 cm) Long, Pendant or Figurine*
Challenge Level: *Advanced*
Origin: *Fusion Tie*

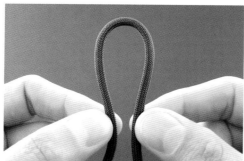

1. At the middle of the cord, make a bight.

2. Rotate the bight into a clockwise loop.

3. Bight the right running end through the loop…

4. …and tighten, leaving a 0.25 (0.64 cm) loop in the Slip Knot made.

5. One inch (2.5 cm) beneath the bottom of the Slip Knot make a clockwise **P** with the left cord.

6. Hook the right running end left, over the loop of the **P**, the "leg" of the **P**, and the left vertical cord above.

7. Then weave it under the top of the **P** and over itself.

8. Now, hook the right running end left over both vertical cords above.

9. Then weave it over the top of the left loop, under the leg of the P, and over the bottom of the left loop.

10. Take the tip of the left running end in hand.

11. Hook it right, weaving it over the left edge of the arching cord, under the left vertical cord…

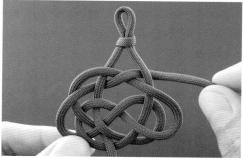

12. …over the top of the arching cord, and under the right vertical cord.

13. Continue forward, weaving the running end over, under…

14. …over, and under the cords beneath it.

15. Take the tip of the left running end in hand.

16. Weave it under, over, under, and over the cords left of the right standing end.

17. Take the tip of the right running end in hand.

18. Weave it over, under, over, and under the cords left of the left standing end.

19. Hook the right running end left, weaving it under and over the cords inside the top right crook.

20. Continue forward, weaving the running end under and over the cords diagonally down and left of the top right crook.

21. Hook the top left running end right, weaving it over and under the cords outside the top left crook.

22. Continue forward, weaving the running end over and under the cords diagonally down and right of the top left crook.

23. Hook the left running end right, weaving it under and over the cords inside the middle left crook.

24. Continue forward, weaving the running end under and over the cords diagonally up and right of the middle left crook.

25. Then hook the running end right, under, over…

26. …and under the cords outside the bottom right crook.

27. Hook the top right running end left. Then weave it over and under the cords outside the middle right crook.

28. Continue forward, weaving the running end over and under the cords diagonally up and left of the middle right crook.

29. Then hook the running end left, over and under the cords inside the bottom left crook.

30. Hook the right running end left, over and under the cords outside the bottom right crook.

31. Continue forward, weaving the running end over, under…

32. …over, and under the cords diagonally up and left of the bottom right crook.

33. Hook the bottom left running end right, over and under the cords inside the bottom left crook.

34. Continue forward, weaving the running end over, under…

35. …over, and under the cords diagonally up and right of the bottom left crook.

36. Then hook the running end left, over and under the cords above.

37. Flip the piece over, horizontally.

38. Cross the running ends, right cord over left.

39. Bight the left running end until 1.5 in. (3.8 cm) long and tuck it under the top left crook.

40. Bight the right running end until 1.5 in. (3.8 cm) long and tuck it under the top right crook.

Paracord Critters

41. Bight the left running end until 1 in. (2.5 cm) long and tuck it under the bottom left crook.

42. Bight the right running end until 1 in. (2.5 cm) long and tuck it under the bottom right crook.

43. Cross the running ends, left cord over right.

44. Then tuck the right running end under and over the cord above it.

45. Cross the running ends, right cord over left.

46. Then tuck the left running end under and over the cord above it.

47. Tighten the Square Knot made, firmly.

48. Tuck the running ends under the bottom middle crook.

49. Flip the piece over, horizontally.

50. Shape the Sea Turtle's shell until arched and its flippers until bent back.

51. Leave the running ends uncut for a Sea Turtle Necklace…

52. …or carefully snip and singe the running ends at their base, to make a Sea Turtle Figurine.

About the Author

J.D. Lenzen is the creator of the highly acclaimed YouTube channel *Tying It All Together* (youtube.com/tyingitalltogether), and the producer of over 350 instructional videos. He's been formally recognized by the International Guild of Knot Tyers (IGKT) for his contributions to knotting, and is the originator of fusion knotting—the creation of innovative knots and ties through the merging of different knot elements or knotting techniques. *Paracord Critters* (PC) is Lenzen's fifth knot instruction book. *Decorative Fusion Knots* (DFK), *Paracord Fusion Ties - Volume 1* (PFT-V1), *Paracord Fusion Ties - Volume 2* (PFT-V2), and *Paracord Project Inspirations* (PPI) are also available. He lives and works in San Francisco, California.

© Ash Gerry

Other 4th Level Indie Books

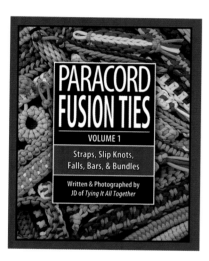

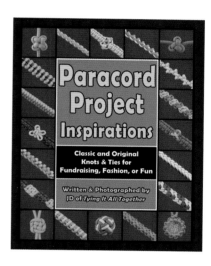

Paracord Fusion Ties - Volume 1
Straps, Slip Knots, Falls, Bars, & Bundles

ISBN: 978-0-9855578-0-5
8" x 10" Softcover

Published 2012

Paracord Fusion Ties - Volume 2
Survival Ties, Pouches, Bars, Snake Knots, & Sinnets

ISBN: 978-0-9855578-3-6
8" x 10" Softcover

Published 2013

Paracord Project Inspirations
Classic and Original Knots & Ties for Fundraising, Fashion, or Fun

ISBN: 978-0-9855578-6-7
8" x 10" Softcover

Published 2014